Flippity

Fluppity

Flop

Flippity Fluppity Flop

Nonsense rhymes and Flip book

for the young at heart.

Bean Sprout Press

Mike Johnson   **Daniela Gast**

Bean Sprout Press,
an imprint of Lasavia Publishing Ltd.
Auckland, New Zealand

©Poems: Mike Johnson, 2021
©Art: Daniela Gast, 2021

This book is copyright. Apart from any fair dealing for the purpose of private study, research, criticism or reviews, as permitted under the Copyright Act, no part may be reproduced by any process without the permission of the publishers.

ISBN 978-1-9911519-0-2

Dedication

This fun book is dedicated first to Mike's youngest grandchildren, Aka Johnson, Mikassi Moon Reihana and Sailor Sky Reihana. Also to, Tomas Oliver Johnson, Henry Michael Johnson, Saxon Johnson Carter, Marlon Grover and Lexie Rackham. Also to these little scranglers: Alva, Alba, Pan, Noah, Bethan, Bricie, Alley, Aeris, Max, Irena, Lore, Kalle, Danka, Alma, Arrow, Tara Lilly, Luky, Herbert and Sophie.

Author's Notes – Nonsense Rhymes

For young children it begins with the sounds of words, and the delight of those sounds. Sounds come before meaning. Delight comes before sense. Silly nonsense turns into fun.

These little poems sound good read aloud by an adult or older child, as their true audience is children who have not yet learned to read or are just learning. Simplicity reigns, and the rhythms are often based on familiar chants or nursery rhymes, making it easy for those reading aloud to pick it up.

Nonsense poems are a much-neglected genre, but survive in our nursery rhymes, and in the work of some rare poets like A A Milne, who is an inspiration for this work. They are trickier than they look, as they can be as silly as, but not stupid. They can be surreal and bizarre, but not scary, at least too scary. They can allude to situations, but must not attempt to teach. And above all, they have to work as little songs, almost, with fun rhymes to hold them together.

Children are natural absurdists, with a ready sense of humour that we often overlook, and a delight in whimsy we adults might envy. Children are always happy to laugh. It's a healthy sign of a developing intelligence. My trust is that there is something in here that will tickle their fancy.

And if there seems to be adult implications slipping through here and there, to be appreciated by the dedicated parent or caregiver alone, well, they deserve it. I plead innocence. You don't have to be a child to appreciate a bit of light-hearted nonsense.

A heartfelt thanks to Clyde and Wendy Watson for their inspirational *Father Fox's Pennyrhymes*. Published in 1976, this is a classic of the genre, and without it this book could not have been written. I've adopted some of their rhythms and structures for this work, and for that I give full acknowledgement.

Mike Johnson, Waiheke Island 2021

Artist's Note

I always loved flip books, or thumb cinema (Daumenkino), as we call them in Germany, the oldest and simplest form of animation. At school I would animate a bouncing ball on the corner of my exercise book. There is something magical about flip books, static simple images come to life.

Daniela Gast, 2021

the big why

Why is the sky so blue, so blue
why are the hills so brown
why does it seem
to lose all the green
when leaves fall to the ground
the ground
when leaves fall to the ground?

Why is the sky so sometimes,
how is the moon so yet
why does the cloud look like a shroud
why are the stars so set, so set
why are the stars so set?

I like a sometimes sky at night
I like a moon that's true
I like a cloud to speak out loud
and stars that are properly blue
blue blue
stars that are properly blue

I cry when the toybox is empty
I laugh when it is full
I make a face to create the space
and set up the push-and-pull
pull pull
to set up the push-and-pull

so paint the gate
with a shade that's late
and colour the springtime early

Oh!

Why is the sky so blue, so blue
why are the hills so brown
why do they all seem
to lose all the green
when leaves fall to the ground
the ground

when leaves fall to the ground?

Nothing comes of nothing

Nothing is a funny word
I don't know what it means,
since nothing must mean nothing
there is nothing to be seen.

Nothing is a nothing word
which puzzles me a lot,
I don't know what it means
and I don't know what it's got.

But since it is a nothing word
with nothing found inside
nothing can't be something
so nothing's there to hide.

Oh nothing is as nothing
it's as quiet as a mouse
nothing speaks to no onany kind of no one
and nothing lives with nothing
in a nothing sort of house.

Funny

It's funny what I dream
when I'm dreaming that I'm dreaming,

when I'm dreaming what I'm dreaming
what I dream what I am.

It's funny what I am when I'm dreaming
what I am when I'm dreaming

what I am
when I dream.

Fire fire burning bright

Here's a fire
burning bright,
wood to ash
and ash to light.

Here's the smoke
thick and tight,
yellow to black
and day to night.

Wisdom

There's wisdom in the parlour,
there's wisdom in the pot;
there's wisdom in the gravy
and maybe there's not.

Oh poplar trees stand up tall
rhododendrons squat, roses crawl,
and each to every, all to all
there's wisdom in the pot.

There's wisdom in the garden,
there's wisdom on the grass;
there's wisdom in the moment
and wisdom in the past.

Oh I could show you wisdom
if I could find a little bit
that wasn't part of something else
that wasn't really **IT**.

**But there's wisdom in the parlour,
there's wisdom in the pot;
there's wisdom in the gravy
and maybe there's not.**

One little match-head

Little red match-head
sitting on a stick,

watch that match-head
quick! quick! quick!

When it flares brightly
it may burn your hand,

one little red match-head
burns up the land.

Mr Wolfie

Mr Wolfie knows the time
he's got it on his wrist,
and if you happen to ask him it
he'll put you on his list.

He is a smooth talker
his watch is very flash,
he has a word for everything
and matches it with cash.

I'd keep and eye on Wolfie, friend
I'd let him know you know,
and when he starts his smooth fast talk
I'd turn around and go.

Yes, Mr Wolfie knows the time
he'll tell you quick as look,
and if you don't move on fast
he'll put you in his book.

Four little kittens

Four little kittens
lying in a heap

four little kittens
do nothing but sleep

sleep and drink
and drink and sleep,

four little kittens
lying in a heap.

I wish

The sea is the sea
is the endless sea
stretching from side to side

it stretches so far
from the rocks to the star
however could it be so wide?

Oh I wish I could go sailing,
I wish I was on the sea,
I'd bring back a fish,
I'd bring back a wish
and cook for you and me.

Here comes the flood

Here comes the flood!
Here comes the flood!

The streets are filled with
streaming mud.

That is the sound
of a laughing hound

move everybody to higher ground!

Christmas pudding

The banker and the businessman
the sailor and the cat
set out to sea one day
in an oversized bowler hat.

They sailed off to an island
and sat on a coral reef
to eat their Christmas pudding
and to clean their teeth.

Mean Jean

Mean Jean
she's long and lean

she sounds just like
a washing machine,

with eyes like kites
and a nose that bites

she's a mean Jean
when she gets up steam,

Mean Jean
she's long and lean.

Take me for a ride

take me for a ride
on your slide slide slide
take me for a ride on your slide.

Take me for a swing on your
swing swing swing
take me for a swing on your swing.

Take me for a bounce
on your tramp-o-line
your tramp-o-line
take me for a little
bounce bounce bounce.

I'm ready
I'm steady
I'm all set to go.

Oh! take me for a ride
on your slide slide slide
take me for a ride on your slide.

Little Johnny

Little Johnny did
a loop-de-loop,

fell right into
a bowl of soup.

He jumped on a broccoli
and paddled to shore,

went to his mother
and asked for more.

Bugal call

I don't want to get up
I don't want to get up
I don't want to get up in the morning.

I just as soon stay
in bed all day
cuddled up comfortably snoring.

Yellow

I have a yellow canary
that can sing sing sing.

I have a yellow telephone
that can ring ring ring.

Sing canary, sing!
Ring telephone, ring!

Ring yellow!
Sing yellow!

Ring and sing and ring!

Busker

Busker! Busker!
will you play for me?

Busker! Busker!
one two three!

Sing me some words
that I've never heard

take me away
from tomorrow and today

play me a song
and I'll be gone.

Play me fiddle-de-de.

Guitar man

Have you heard
the guitar man
the guitar man
the guitar man;

have you heard the guitar man
who plays in Vulcan Lane?

Flippity fluppity flop

Flippity fluppity flop,
the frog hopped into the shop
the shop
the frog hopped into the shop

but all of the bins
sprouted fins
so out again he did hop
did hop
out again he did
                        hop.

Flippity fluppity flop
the frog hopped out of the shop.

Bread

White flour,
brown flour,
mix it in a bowl

turn it round,
pat it down,
give it a good roll.

Knead it,
pound it,
leave it out to rise

shape it,
bake it
hear the hungry cries!

Colours

Give me red.
Give me blue.

Give me green and orange too.

Saffron yellow
indigo and gold

give me colours that are extra bold.

Pohutukawa

The trees bloom red
and the trees bloom green

up on the cliff face
where they lean.

Spark out the red!
Spark out the green!

Let the pohutukawa
be seen.

Hop

I saw a kangaroo
go

hop
hop
hop

I saw a little Joey
go

flop
flop
flop

Joey's out
Joey's in
Joey can't be seen

you can't see where he is
only where he's been.

The King of Spain

The king of Spain
got in a plane
and flew all round the world.

When he got there
he sat in a chair
and found himself home again.

Counting

One
is not enough

two
is pretty tough

three
is kind of wee

but four is just the score!

Lippity Lop

Lippity Lop is at sixes and sevens,
he doesn't know if it is nine or eleven;

nine or eleven, eleven or nine,
Lippity Lop is right on time.

Give him a shadow, give him a stick
he'll tell you the time as quick as a flick.

Banging pots

I'm sitting on the kitchen floor
banging all the pots

Bang!
Bang!
Hit the pan!

Bang!
Bang!
There! It rang!

I'm sitting by the kitchen door
banging lots and lots.

Values

The value of sun
is its shining

the value of air
is our breath.

You can measure a log
by the cost of a frog

and forget
about all the rest.

Snail in a pail

Here's my
snail

in a
pail.

Tuck it
in a bucket

half filled up with
grass.

Oh let us think

Oh let us think of returning
over the fields of play,
oh let us think of linking hands
and stepping back through May.

I've no one to account to,
I've no one by my side;
I tried to stop
the silly old mop
and found no place to hide.

So I am a little melancholy
as you can see,
I've been too busy wondering
if I am me.

A twist of fire makes the rose,
takes the rose's name;
they twist on up towards the gate
with a single flame.

I'd like to follow with them,
I'd like to go their way;
I wish I could go riding
through the fields of play.

Oh let us think of returning
over the fields of play,
oh let us think of linking hands
and stepping back through May.

One is for

One is for my mother
always on the go

two is for my father
with the lawns to mow

three is for my sister
who's neither here nor there

and four is for my brother
with the dreadlock hair.

Poems

At home I have a book of poems
right by my bed,

and every night
one or two poems get read.

Now I've got these poems
floating in my head.

Running

Give me a hill where I can run free
oh give me a hill to run on.

I'll run with the moon and I'll run
with the sun
and I'll run with the run with the
run-on.

Give a hill where I can be me
oh give me a hill to run on.

I'll run with the many, I'll run
with the one
and I'll run with the run with the
run-on.

Give me a hill where I'm free to be free
oh give me a hill to run on.

Little man

I had a little man
I could fit in my pocket,
I had a little man no bigger
than a locket.

We went to market
and he danced a jig.
I bought a doll's house,
he bought a fig.

It's funny when you see
the games he plays,
he's a funny little man
with funny little ways.

Wishbone

I've got the wishbone
to split in two,

a half for me
and a half for you.

I'll get the bigger half
you'll get the small,

I'll get the wish
and wish for us all.

A loan

I got a loan
from Aunty Joan
said I'd return it on Sunday.

Some was spent
and some was lent
and I won't have any till Monday!

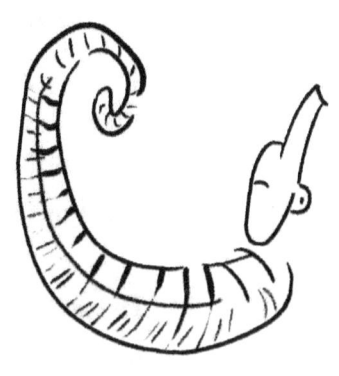

Humpty Dumpty

I've got a Humpty Dumpty,
he's not upon a wall

I've got a Humpty Dumpty
he'll never ever fall.

I will not need king's horses.
I will not need king's men.

I'll never have to put Humpty
back together again.

The best gift

I've got a little gift for you,
I've kept it all this time;

it's a funny little something
that I wish was mine.

Oh you can have fine turquoise.
You can have dull gold.

You can have warm rubies
and diamonds crisp and cold,

but you would miss this little gift
of mine,

you wouldn't have this funny something
this little gift of rhyme

A-hundred-and-one

A hundred-and-one dalmatians
went for a run in the park,
a hundred-and-one dalmatians
suddenly lost their bark.

They saw a thousand cats
dressed in spats
their eyes yellow and dark.

A hundred-and-one dalmatians
made a run for a gate,
a hundred-and-one dalmatians
not a one was late.

They saw a thousand cats
dressed in spats
and that was the end of that

I'd like to hear a story

I like to hear a story
before I go to bed;

Cinderella, Thumbelina
all the ones I've read.

I love Peter Pan
and the Vanishing Man
and the cow that couldn't say zed.

I make Thumbelina fat,
Cinderela slow
and Pinocchio's nose won't grow.

I like to hear a story
before I go to bed;
I like to change it all around
and stand it on its head.

Tell me a tale

Tell me a tale of yesterday,
tell me tale of yore

give me a story
with blood
and with gory

tell me tale of yore.

Tomorrow will set the world dreaming,
tomorrow will waltz to the door,

but give me a story
with blood
and with gory

tell me a tale of yore.

Dilly-dally

Dilly-dally, shilly-shally
tell me something very smelly.

There was a man whose name was Cox
who fried and ate his old work socks.

Thrush and Tui

Thrush has a loud song,
so does tui.

Tui goes for ding-dong,
thrush holds a hui.

Weta party

Have you heard?
Have you heard?

The wetas all have
passed the word,

they will party, it is said
this very night, upon your bed.

Have you heard?
Have you heard?

the wetas all have
passed the word.

Tonight, it's said
upon your bed!

(( ))

Come over

Come over and be my Special Friend,
we'll talk and play without end.

Climb the fence, climb the gate
we'll make a date for half-past eight.

We can meet and have tea
at exactly half-past three

with ice cream, cake, and something more
around about half-past four.

When it comes to five
we'll jive
we'll jive and jive and jive
and jive!

Come over and be my Special Friend,
we'll talk and play without end.

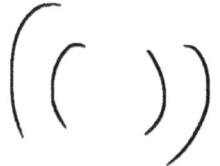

Flying saucers

Tell me, tell me,
when you look into the air
have you seen the saucers there?

They say they're like two plates
stuck together
just flying around
making a creepy kind of
swishing sound

with mysterious lights
that come and go
sometimes fast
sometimes slow.

There's people inside, so they say
from another place
another space.

As for me, I don't know
I've never seen one, they're shy of me,
they just won't show

but what about you?
What've you seen
up in the sky?

Have you seen the saucers fly?

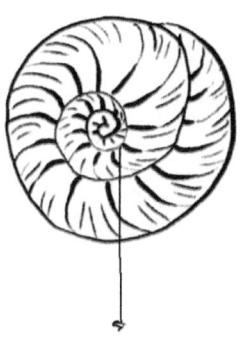

Mrs Moon

Mrs Moon, I've heard say
creeps in to steal the sun away,

but when at night I look up
I see the sun in a moon-filled cup.

I can't believe every word
of every story that I've heard!

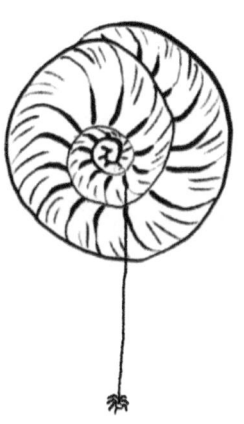

Jenny

Jenny jumps through
the hoop,
Jenny skips round
the loop

Jenny goes over the edge of the bars
and comes back
with a swoop.

What does the taniwha look like?

Nobody knows
the shape of his nose
the cast of his toes.

Nobody knows
just how far his tail goes.

Not a fearsome beast
not a handsome warrior
not a noble priest
not a bird
not a word
not a worthy feast

I'd like to see a tawiwha
then I'd tell you straight
if his feet are two
his eyes are six
or if his heads are eight.

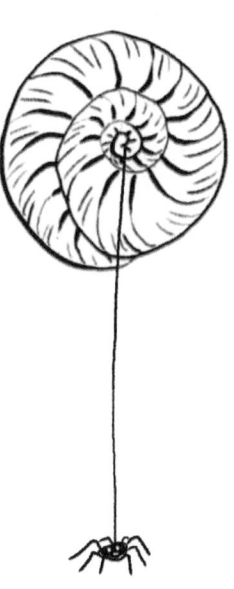

Till that day we have to say
the monster is unknown

and go to sleep and see in dreams
the shape that he has shown.

For nobody knows
nobody knows
the cut of his clothes
the big suppose
nobody knows

just how far his tail goes.

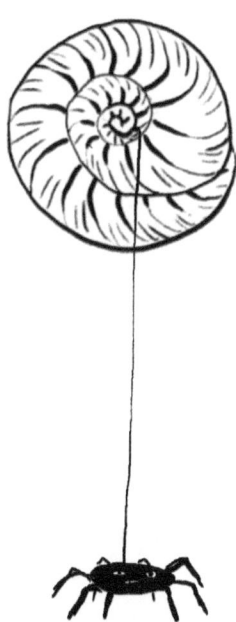

Before

Let me down soft and easy
let me down super slow
let me down sleepways gently
into the satiny snow.

Hold me just for a moment
hold me super slow
hold me while I slip away

before you turn and go.

Hot buttered scones!

Hot buttered scones!
    all soft and runny

Hot buttered scones!
    dripping with honey

Hot buttered scones!
    tasting super yummy

Hot buttered scones!
    safe inside my tummy

Flying

Once around the loopity-loop
once around the kowhai,
once around the Nursery Rhyme
down with the hot pie.

Every time I swing my hoop
someone breaks up crying,
now I'm dizzy all the time
I think I'm flying.

Frost

frost is tinkly
frost is crinkly
frost is stiff and bright

frost is shiny
frost is rhymey
frost is clean and white

frost is misty
frost is ghosty
frost comes in the night

Jerd and the word

Jerd the Nerd
heard the word
and took it for a walk.

He walked it to
he walked it fro
he walked it forward and aft,
and everywhere he walked it
the people came and laughed.

Jerd the Nerd
lost the word
somewhere between breakfast and dinner,
he came to grief in a great relief
and decided that he was the winner.

Certain Bear

Where are you Certain Bear,
Are you hiding far or near?

Certain Bear if you can hear,
do not fear, do not fear.

When night comes, you must be
by my dreaming head,

cuddled up beside me
in my own certain bed

Hi! ho! he!

Hi! ho! he!
The wasp shall marry the bee,
the slug will tug
with the bug in the rug
and the ants will run off with the flea
the flea
the ants will run off with the flea.

Hi! ho! he!
The wasp has married the bee,
the slug with the bug
took the rug for a hug
and the ants ran off with the flea
the flea
the ants ran off with the flea.

Distances

Down at Bluff
the people are tough
and even the sheep wear mittens.

But in Whangarei
the people all say
the sun's not hot it's kittens

What is?

What is sweeter than sweet?
What is rounder than round?
What is closer than close?
What is stronger than strong?
What is nicer than nice?
What is dearer than dear?
What is bluer than blue?

Love is sweeter than sweet.
Love is bigger than big.
Love is rounder than round.
Love is closer than close.
Love is stronger than strong.
Love is nicer than nice.
Love is dear than dear.
Love is bluer than blue.

Wiggily piggily

Wiggily piggily
steak and egg pie,
jiggerly joggerly
just you and I.

With a little pinch of this
and a little pinch of that,
a little tad of poddle-soup
from a witch's hat.

Add a piece of doggy-poo
and a mozzy's wing,
to a dob of yukky-yuk
and a yokkily thing.

Boil them up together
stir them with a spoon,
then you'll have a smelly spell
and a moony tune.

Wiggily piggily
steak and egg pie,
jiggerly joggerly
just you and I.

Swallow it all down!

Broccoli, cabbage
potato and leek.

Carrot, parsley
and kumera to eat.

These are my vegetables
I'd rather put aside

for ice cream and chocolate
and a lollipop ride.

But Mummy says I have to
and Daddy just frowns

so I'll trick them with a teaspoonfull
and swallow it down!

Little Master Muffin

Little Master Muffin
came into town.
Little Master Muffin
laid the law down.

Little Master Muffin
puffed out his chest.
Little Master Muffin
always knows what's best.

One day Mummy warned him,
she told him to take care;
she said there was a bogey man
who looked just like a bear.

The bogeyman would get him,
would eat him up for sure,
but Little Master Muffin laughed
(it sounded like a roar).

No bogeyman for me, he cried
and slipped upon the step
where the bogeyman was waiting
with his bogey-bogey net.

Alas for Master Muffin
who surely had his day;
Bogey put him in a sack
and carried him away.

But sometimes if you listen hard
you can hear him call,
'I'm Little Master Muffin
and I'm master of you all!'

My drawing wouldn't stay

I tried to draw a drawing
but my drawing wouldn't stay.

It wriggled
and jumped,
it rumpled
and bumped
and flew into a rage.

I tried to draw a drawing
but my drawing wouldn't stay.

It wriggled
and it jiggled
and it jumped
                         right off the page!

A monster with a rock

When I go to sleep on the
ground ground ground

I listen very hard to the
sound sound sound.

There's a monster with a rock
talking without stop

and a wormy wormy worm
that goes round round round.

Mary Mouse

Mary Mouse is very busy
sweeping out the house,

sweeping spiders, sweeping toys,
sweeping everything else.

Sweep goes the broom,
Sweep! Sweep! Sweep!

Everybody listen.
Everyone stand still.
There's Mary Mouse a-sweeping,
she's a-sweeping with a will.

Swish goes the broom,
Swish! Swish! Swish!

Sweeping spiders, sweeping toys
sweeping everything else.

I wish I had a broom like hers
to sweep with Mary Mouse!

Run, run, run

Run for the ferry!
Run for the bus!
Run against the clock
make a lot of fuss.

That's what my **Daddy** does
my **Mummy** does too,
running to the running hands
just to make do.

Sometimes I'm very quiet.
Sometimes I'm toottle-to.
And sometimes I make **A GREAT BIG FUSS**
'cos I'm running too.

Meet me in the garden

Meet me in the garden
meet me on the path,
meet me by the little porch
meet me at the hearth.

Meet me on the skyway
where the world begins,
meet me on the starway
where the earth spins.

Meet me here.
Meet me there.
We'll meet wherever we please!
We'll dance among the flower heads
we'll scratch amid the fleas.

I know a certain someone
who meets me everywhere,
a someone sort of someone
who doesn't seem to care

when we meet or how we meet
or if we meet at all!
A meeting sort of someone
I've drawn upon my wall.

Happy flappy

Happy flappy, happy time,
I'm going to sing a happy rhyme
I'm going to clap my hands
to a happy song of mine.

Why am I so happy?
You can ask!
You can ask!

Why am I so flappy
with my arms
arms
      arms?

If you can keep a secret
till the end
        end
                end

If you can keep a secret
and not   bend
         bend
   bend
I will tell youi why I'm happy,
why I'm extra happy-flappy,
let me whisper that I'm going,
oh I'm going, yes I'm going,
I'm going up the road to see
My
      friend
 friend   friend

A tricky little thing

When I run
I run
I run
I run
I run
I run

and when I walk
I walk
I walk
I walk
I walk
I walk

but when I sing
I make just a little-little sound

so small my breath
can hardly make it round.

One day I'll sing
and run
and sing
and run
and sing

I haven't learnt
the trick yet,

it's a tricky little
thing.

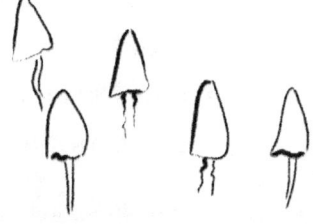

My Mummy

Mummy won't ever listen.
Mummy won't ever hear.

Mummy can't say two-and-six
unless I'm near.

Mummy is a ratbag
Mummy is a geek.
Instead of a nice huggle
there's a peck upon the cheek.

Sometimes Mummy goes away
sometimes she comes back.
Sometimes I'm all alone
and sometimes I'm not.

But when I want my Mummy
there's lots of tears to come
for my Mummy is my Mummy
and I'm her little one.

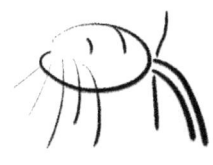

Ladybird

I have a little ladybird
that crawls across the leaf.

She's a hungry little ladybird
that eats
and eats
and eats.

She eats the aphid, eats the mite
and eats the beetles too.

She eats the little creatures that
would eat the leaf right through.

I love my little ladybird
I call her Hungry Jane

for when she's finished eating
she starts to eat again.

Bird in the sky

Bird in the sky
with its flappy-flappy wings,

how do we hear
when the bird sings?

With our ear we hear
inside of our head,

where little fine bones
lie on their bed.

Bird in the sky
that sweetly sings,

how do we see
the rush of your wings?

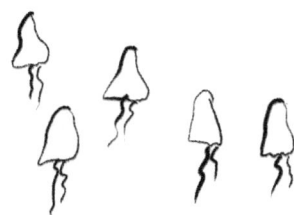

With an eye we spy
at the back of our face

where nerves slip together
as webby as lace.

www.ingramcontent.com/pod-product-compliance
Lightning Source LLC
Chambersburg PA
CBHW021445070526
44577CB00002B/268